I
don't
need
to
know
your
name
to
be
your
friend

I don't need to know your name to be

FORTRESS PRESS · PHILADELPHIA

CONRAD WEISER

your friend

Library of Congress Catalog Card Number 72-75658

ISBN 0-8006-0124-6

Designed by Otto Reinhardt

The photo on page 115 is by Bill Gray. All others, including
the cover photos are the work of Dick Clapper and his camera.

3229F72   Printed in the United States of America   1-124

read this first

The exercises and simulations in this book have been chosen for their simplicity. This does not mean that valid learning cannot result from their use, but rather that they are "safe." When people are dealing with feelings, it is important that expert guidance be available, and that great care is used. People are not objects to be manipulated at the will of a leader who wants neat things to happen. An individual will involve himself only as much as he is willing and able. To expect anything more would be manipulative. Groups, like individuals, will also set the level of operation in which they feel most comfortable. No leader can force his group to learn things they are not prepared to learn. It would be devious to even try.

Become familiar with the structure and content of the book before you make any decisions about the best use of it for you. It is intended to function for you. You can use it to best advantage only after you have felt its flow and structure.

If you have had no experience or only limited experience with small groups, the book can serve you well by providing helps and specifics for getting groups started on any task. If you are trained and experienced in group work, you will find exercises which will serve as springboards for your own creativity. Modify, modify, modify. Use it. Read it. Play with it. Let the words and your mind work together.

I don't need to know your name to be your friend.

I don't need to know if you're married. I don't need to know how old you are. I don't need to know where you work. I don't need to know where you live. I only need to know if you are a man or a woman, and how much you want to get to know me.

Do you care? Are you ever afraid? What are you afraid of? What do you like to do? Can I do it with you? I'll tell you how you can help me and what I need. I'll tell you my joys, I'll tell you my sorrows. I'll tell you where I live inside and the spirits I am carrying.

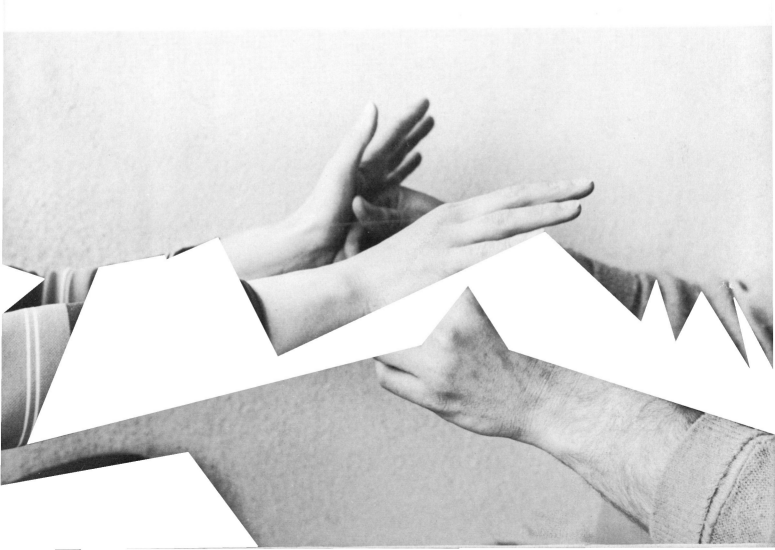

I want to know how you feel.

What your face is like. What your hands are like. How do I feel to you? We'll look at the bright corners first, and then, if we want to and care to, we'll look into the darkest corners, the secret places.

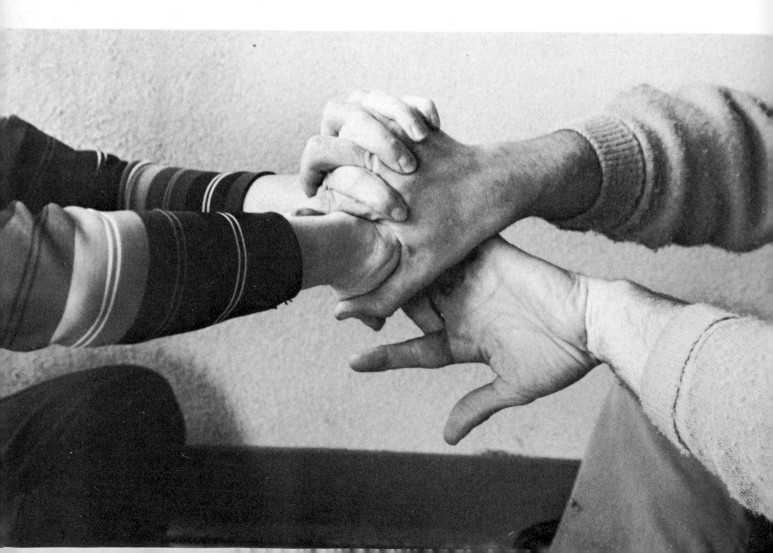

We'll look where we both want to look,

because we can't look anywhere except together. If we are not together, we are not.

If we are together, I want to know your name so I can tell other people I love about meeting you and how much it meant to me. I'll tell you my name and you can do the same.

But I don't need to know your name

to be your friend. You only need to want me to be one.

contents

TIP-TAP-TOUCH

WIN/LOSE

LOSE/LOSE

CONTROL/INTIMACY

list of exercises

LIST OF EXERCISES

WIN/WIN

PLAY (because it's fun)

Introduction

Like most people in my generation, I am more proficient at a win/lose style of life than I am at helping my brother to win. I am more ready to put him down than hold him up. It is easier for me to say "I am what I am" and let it go at that. I would like very much for the world to accommodate itself to me at the moment. Otherwise there are so many unknowns. At least I know where I am and wish that those around me would know it, too. Based on this life-style which assumes that where I am is the most important thing in the universe, I would very much like the world to shape itself around me.

This book seeks to indicate that a competitive, win/lose approach to life and each other is ultimately destructive to the fabric of personal and interpersonal life together. It further seeks to establish a more constructive norm for interpersonal behavior which is win/win. This norm requires that each man use all his strength to lift up and hold up the other because he trusts that the other is doing the same for him. There is no attempt to undermine the joy of struggle, but that struggle helps both parties to win. It is only the struggle to defeat others in order to affirm selfhood that is being attacked.

Competition, we are told, is part of the very backbone of our culture. From an early age, children are conditioned to compete with their peers. Parents tell their children that they are good or bad, behaved or misbehaved by comparing their behavior with that of other children in an unhealthy way. The public schools continue the process by grading students. Pupils are rated in relationship to other children. The Little League also fosters the image that selfhood is determined largely by the comparison of a child to other children. By the time a child reaches adolescence the process has been pretty well completed and an individual believes that life is a win/lose situation. Generation after generation of adults continue to spread the message that win/lose competition is a necessary part of life, and the myth that *you* are the *best* only when you have defeated a significant number of other persons continues. The child who plays Monopoly with great gusto is only a short step away from becoming the adult who plays Bridge with a vengeance.

Given the existing cultural norm, we can assume that when groups of people gather together the likelihood is that each participant wants to "win." Three kinds of interchange occur: Tip-Tap-Touch, Win/Lose, and Lose/Lose.

Tip-Tap-Touch is that hesitant interchange when groups of people are together for the first time. Shyness, reticence, braggadocio, and laughter all mix together in a gigantic cover-up for the more intense competitive interrelating which will follow in any group growth and life together. Win/Lose is first in the sequence of intense relationships. It is self-explanatory. Lose/Lose, a less familiar term, is that negative interrelating which simply means "If I can't get what I want, then you are not going to get what you want, either." Win/Lose and Lose/Lose are where most groups are at the beginning. This is probably somehow related to what individuals see when they look inside themselves.

The interpersonal giant step from these negatively competitive styles begins by facing Control questions squarely and confronting the issues of who is in charge and why do you need to be in charge. Only when these questions are dealt with effectively can persons move toward Intimacy together. The process is a linear one and cannot be short-circuited. The struggle brings the growth. The step begins with "I am what I am; please support me when you can and forgive me when

you must." It does not stop there. Next an individual needs to be able to say, "You are what you are."

The second statement is much more difficult to say than the first. Because now I need to consider what you really want and what you have to say. You may not always be what I want you to be. I need to learn to trust that you are not trying to control me in the sense that someone's always winning and someone's losing. I need to trust that you will not smother me with your needs. I need to know that you will not "love me to pieces" because I'm really not certain what the pieces are all the time. I want to know how I will react, but I won't be afraid to hear it. I'll even try to bend myself so we can fit a little better. Maybe we can take the giant step together. I am what I am and you are what you are. I will try to accommodate myself to you, trusting you will do the same.

Then we can play. When was the last time we walked in the rain together?

Win/Win and Play (because it's fun) is the goal for group life. The arrival at that point requires struggle, pain, and release. It takes a turning inside out. Win/Win means in this context the process of using all your strength to lift up and hold up the other person because you trust that the other person is doing the same. As the content indicates, when this point is reached it is possible to truly play, just because it's fun. No games with winners and losers, good feelings and bad feelings, just play. Flying kites, or whistling grass between your fingers, or dancing in the kitchen on Saturday morning.

This book will help groups of different sizes in the struggle from Tip-Tap-Touch through Control to Intimacy and Play (because it's fun). Participants can be helped to better determine how they can work together effectively. The exercises and simulations will help groups see where they are, get away from where they were, and get together in order to better accomplish the task at hand.

The contents of the book can function in any of three primary settings. First, they will provide a way of getting large task-oriented groups together, so that they can work in smaller groups and accomplish the task. A second setting would be the smaller groups of eight to fifteen members. They may have gathered for any of several purposes and need some way of discovering enough about themselves to tackle the task. A third and perhaps the most exciting setting is in a home. A small group of three to eight persons may gather for the express purpose of knowing each other more deeply.

The sensitive leader will choose an exercise or simulation that will most help his group prepare themselves for the task at hand. Only the leader knows his group and can make the final decision.

Concerning the poetry, prose, songs, and other miscellaneous pieces, they are intended to be read out loud relative to the place where the group is. Obviously, they can be read by individuals as they compare the pieces with the record of their own life. The process described in the book was not one cleverly created to divide a book into neat chapters. It is a process that we are all involved in. We are also at different places.

More than anything else, the creative pieces are a record of my own progress, or lack of it, as I struggle continually to reach out, and touch the sun and the faces of those I love.

The section called Again will come as no surprise to anyone who has worked through the process. It simply implies that anyone who thinks that he's made it and has his house in order, has forgotten the parable of the evil spirits. When the house is swept and clean the demon flies around the world seeking a place to rest. Finding none he returns, bringing with him seven more even more vicious than himself. Anyone who thinks they are *there* . . . BEWARE.

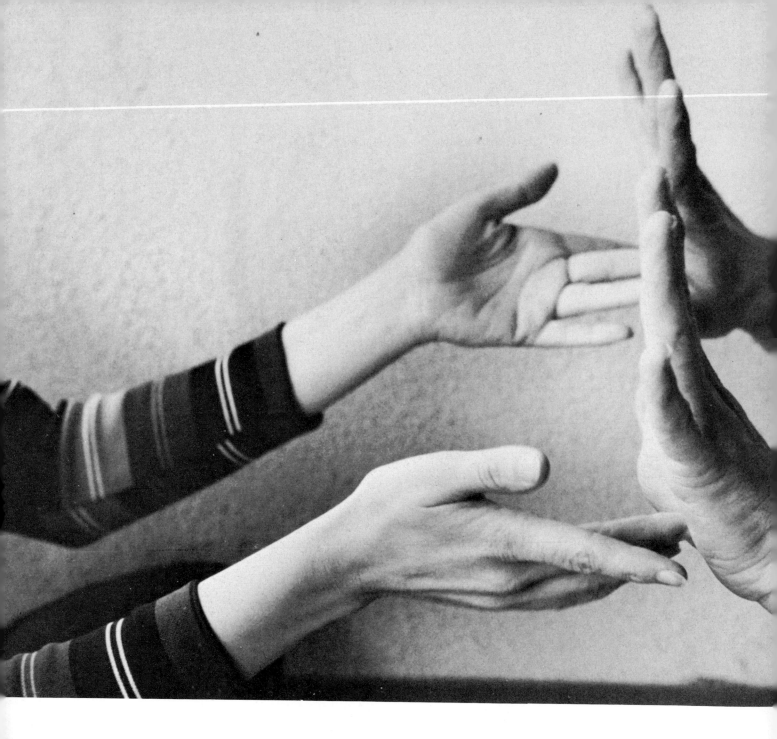

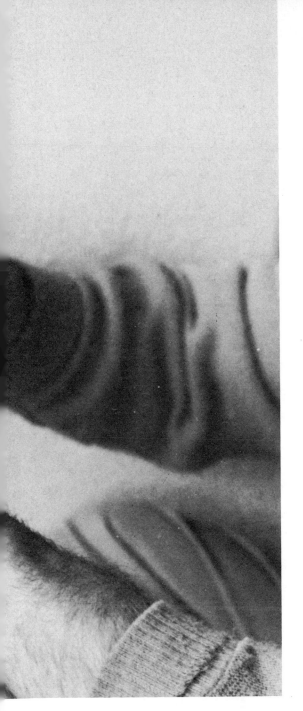

tip-tap-touch

how do I look?

Groups of any size can get some insights into their behavior with each other. Individuals pair with a person whom they do not know at all, or would like to get to know better. Have the partners tell each other one thing they do not like about themselves. When they have done this, ask them to tell each other one thing they genuinely like about themselves.

Ask the group members which they found easier to do. For most, it is easier to identify what is wrong with themselves than what is right. Have the partners discuss this phenomenon. If I don't like me, how do I think that others are going to react to me? Allow about 10 minutes for the discussion.

Conclude by having each partner tell the other one thing they really like about the other person.

the bag thing

This exercise can be used to form small working groups from a larger group. It is valuable in *any* size group for getting to know each other. The multiplication principle is applicable with other exercises in this book. In almost any exercise two or three people who are beginning to get to know each other can pair with other groups of two or three and discuss with each other the impact and learnings of the experience. Two or three pair with another two or three forming working groups of four or six. If larger working groups are desired, the groups of four or six can pair again making groups of eight or twelve.

MATERIALS NEEDED: Magazines distributed around the room that can be torn apart. Have more on hand than you can possibly use. A paper bag for each participant.

TASK: To find pictures, words, phrases, and colors in the magazines which in summary represent the person you think you are. All the pieces removed from the magazines go into the bag.

PROCEDURE: Each participant takes a lunch-sized bag and selects words, phrases, pictures, and short articles from magazines around the room to put into their bag. The items selected should summarize who you really think you are. Come as close as you can to a summary of yourself as you see it. The items may only reflect the basics, but that's OK. Close the bags.

Each person selects one or two other people whom he does not know very well or at all. The dyads or triads exchange bags and the bag holder draws an animal on the outside of the person's bag he received which best symbolizes the other person as he sees him.

Return the bag to the owner and talk about why the animal was chosen. Then open the bags and compare the inside and the outside of each member's bag.

Each small group selects another small group which consists of people they do not know very well. Group and share the experience with each other. How was it? What was learned? What can we say about first impressions? Did the animal selected say anything about the basis for new relationships?

The new groups of four or six pair with another and form the working groups of eight or twelve. Groups can then discuss what needs to happen for groups to form.

one thing only

Pair by picking a person you don't know or would like to know better. Begin by looking at each other in silence. Take one or two minutes for this. Take another minute in silence to think of the one thing you would like to know about your partner and what one thing you would like to tell your partner about yourself. Do it. Repeat with a different partner until all have been with each other once. If the group is too large, only repeat about five times.

We All Laughed

The first thing that comes to my mind is walking out of the junior high school and beginning the ten-block journey home. Down past the "smoking corner" where the mansion stood. We thought it was a mansion anyway. No one seemed to know who lived there, but the house was surrounded by a high stone wall. I used to stop there every day and bum a cigarette from one of the ninth-graders. We seventh-graders weren't brave enough to walk into Pete's and buy a pack. For me that was particularly understandable because my mother bought all her groceries there. Pete was the kind of a nice guy who would call her and say, "Bill was in today and bought a pack of Luckies." I just knew he was that kind of a guy.

I remember the day I didn't stop. None of my friends did either. I even walked on the other side of the street because some "colored" kids were standing around smoking and laughing. We all knew that they "hung together" and preferred it that way. Everyone knew that. I never wondered who everyone was. Who was I to question the validity of so formidable a number as "everyone."

When I think back there was more, lots more. It only begins to make sense in retrospect. Like so many other things that take their meaning with a backward glance.

There was the first band. Me . . . the white kid. Cadillac, Otis, Herman, and "Fats." Those were the big days of Fats Domino and every black kid over two hundred pounds fit the image and seemed content with the designation. Cadillac's name was really Dodge. His father was a minister and Dodge was the name he chose for his son. But "Cadillac" was the name he had painted on the drum with a big gold V, so Cadillac it was.

There was the black man who rode in the back of the pick-up. He had gray hair and was one of the few genuinely friendly strangers I ever met. I was shocked when he spoke Pennsylvania Dutch.

There were the band trips to Washington when the black kids stayed in one hotel and we stayed in another. I wondered why, and then laughed because I was certain that their accommodations couldn't have been any worse than ours.

There was a lot more. Like every other white man, I don't have to think very hard in retrospect to see and feel the racism of our past and present which rises to haunt the comfortable evenings spent with my family.

One of the many jobs I had was with a trucking company in my hometown. Come to think of it, there were no blacks working there even though the town had a large percentage of non-whites. But when I was there, I never noticed.

One day I remember was very hot. It was even hotter at the job because the whole surrounding area was macadam.

An old bus pulled in and stopped. Being basically the kind of a kid who would just as soon loaf as work, I walked out to see what was going on. That faded blue bus was the biggest pile of junk I ever saw. The fenders were crumpled, the windows were not all in place, and the back bumper was gone completely. But that wasn't really important.

The door to the bus was open so I walked inside. Man, I thought it was hot outside! It was like an oven inside and the seats were filled with people. They all sat there sweating and not saying a word. They just sat. A bus full of blacks, just sitting and staring. Even the children stared, unmoving.

Brakes squealed outside the bus. A big gold car pulled up beside the blue rubble and a fat man with a big cigar stepped out and walked into the garage. He walked to the foreman's desk and asked my father if the wreck could be kept going. He had a whole busload of migrants and was their agent. How could he get the work if he couldn't produce the labor?

"It'll take about seven hours," my father said.

"Can you patch it enough to run?"

"Just enough, but it won't be safe."

"That's OK. We don't have to go far. Besides, I don't have to ride in it." The fat man laughed, and so did everyone around him, including myself. The customer is always right.

another color thing

Spread magazines around the room. Have the participants, working individually, tear out a color which most closely represents the kind of group to which they would like to belong. Then have the participants group according to color (reds with reds, blues with blues, etc.). Talk about why you chose the color and what it represents to you. Allow 5 minutes for thinking and choosing a color, and about 20 minutes for talking about what that color means to you.

VARIATIONS: 1. Using the same procedure, change the task to "Choose a color which most closely represents your feeling about___." The subject can be almost anything: God, mass media, the church, the world, my job, children, adults. The conversation and dialogue generated by such discussions are fruitful and always a good starter for any group. The danger of this exercise is overkill. Used too often, the response is "Oh, no, another color thing!" This overkill has already happened to collages as an exercise. But if you've never tried either, or have not overused either, try one.

2. THE COLLAGE is a group exercise in which the teams make a collage of pictures, colors, pipe cleaners, or other items which represents your theme. Again, the subject field is limitless.

paper apron

MATERIALS NEEDED: Large piece of newsprint for each participant. Water base magic markers (oil base will go through onto clothes and walls) or crayons for each participant.

PROCEDURE: Each participant writes one thing he wants others to know about him on the newsprint with a magic marker or crayon. Cut a hole in the middle of the sheet like a poncho and put it on. Walk around talking freely to the other participants. After freely exchanging brief conversations, write something you want to say to the other participants about the conversation or something you want to say about them on their newsprint. After everyone has spoken to everyone else, break into groups of two or three, remove the paper ponchos and talk about the comments. What kind of image do you think is being projected by you? How does the person people see compare with the you you understand yourself to be?

trigger sheet

PURPOSE: To bring into focus some of the feelings and ideas that participants have about themselves and others; to provide a glimpse of attitudes at the beginning of a gathering; to provide an encounter for two people who may not know each other.

MATERIALS: List of incomplete sentences duplicated in sufficient quantity; pencils.

MINIMUM TIME: 20 minutes.

SPACE: Conference room.

NUMBER OF PARTICIPANTS: Any number.

WHAT TO LOOK FOR: Degree of willingness to open up and look at one's deeper self.

DETAILS OF THE ACTIVITY: Each phrase on this page begins a sentence which is incomplete but should trigger an idea for completing it. The participant should put down the first thing that pops into his mind. The answers will be particularly helpful in the process of self-discovery.

When it rains I . . .

My mother always . . .

When I go to church I . . .

When I get old I'm going to . . .

My friends feel that I . . .

The trouble with me is . . .

The thing that I do best is . . .

In our home it's usually . . .

Jesus is . . .

I get angry when . . .

When I get home from this meeting I'm .

I especially like . . .

Right now I feel like . . .

I hope this meeting . . .

The person next to me is very . . .

A good definition of myself is . . .

When the group has finished this list have them pair off and alternately respond to each other sentence by sentence. When the set of sentences is completed, discuss their responses and what they think they mean.

This exercise is best suited for groups where getting to know each other is desirable.

If we choose to live in community,
living responsibly with each other
is mandatory.

up against the wall

This exercise will help your group visualize values and engage in lively dialogue about them.

Divide the group into smaller groups of six or eight. Distribute paper and pencils to each participant. In the upper left-hand corner of the paper have each person write his name. In column format under their own name, have them write the names of the other participants in their group. First names will probably be sufficient. The names serve as a reference for the game only and will not be recorded anywhere else.

Across the top of the page write the words AGREE, UNDECIDED, and DISAGREE. This will complete the form for the game. You may want to play several rounds of the game.

As input to set the stage for the game, read *one* of the following statements. Do not discuss the statement. Let the statement set the tone for the game.

1. People with money are a success.

2. Human life is doomed on this planet.

3. War is a good thing sometimes.

4. Patriotism is an old-fashioned issue.

5. People do not need close friends.

6. People should disobey laws they disagree with.

7. Majority rule is the best yet devised.

8. Individuals determine their own destiny.

9. (Use your imagination and devise more statements.)

Begin playing the game by having the participants listen to one of the statements. Allow time for each member of the groups to listen and form an opinion about it. Does the participant agree with the statement?

Each participant is to check one of the spaces behind his name (AGREE, UNDECIDED, or DISAGREE). He is then to check one space behind the name of each other group member indicating how he thinks each person will decide.

After all the participants have reached a personal decision and made a judgment about all the other members of the small group, have them assume their personal positions on an imaginary line which is explained in the following paragraph.

The game involves decision-making and judgment as well as motion on the part of the participants. When each participant has reached a decision, he will be asked to make a physical commitment to his decision. In addition to the decision made by each participant, he will also be asked to decide whether the other members of his group AGREE, DISAGREE, or are UNDECIDED. Imagine that a line has been drawn from one wall of your meeting room to the opposite wall. That is the decision line. Let one wall be the AGREE place. The other end of the line on the opposite wall is the DISAGREE point. The middle is UNDECIDED. Each participant will be moving to the point on the imaginary line which most closely resembles his own decision.

There will be some surprises when the members of the groups move to the point on the imaginary line which most closely resembles their decision. Some significant discussion will ensue about why some persons moved where they did and why others moved where they did. Other discussion will concern judgments made about individuals.

Take the time required to discuss the decisions reached by each of the members. Were there any surprises? What criteria did each member use when making a judgment about the other members? Does lack of evidence have any influence on judgment? Take the time required for members to discuss these questions and their judgments with each other. You may also have members attempt to change other's opinions.

Play the game a second time using another statement. Have the participants return to their seats when the discussion among the members is complete. Read another of the statements and repeat the process. Suggest that a different mark be made on the forms in order to distinguish it from the first one. Are judgments more accurate than they were the first time? Hold a discussion when the participants have moved to their positions. Attempt to change minds.

VARIATION: Emphasize the dialogue about opinions and encourage participants to attempt to change persons at opposite poles, or have those in the UNDECIDED area make up their minds. Keep the discussion lively by using more statements and eliminating the written part.

body tracing

Participants pair off and trace each other on large pieces of white shelf paper or paper table covering. Each person lies down while his partner traces him. You may want to take the time to cut out the forms but this is not necessary. Using crayons or water base felt-tipped pens, fill in both realistically and symbolically what you know about the other person. Words as well as pictures may be used. After this has been done, the partners can talk about what was filled in and fill in additional details about themselves.

The results can be posted on the walls with masking tape, for further reference in residential events. During the course of the event, participants may wish to add details to their tracing.

joy

Joy!

Now there's a word you've got to watch out for. It sort of sneaks up on you and takes you off guard. It means something specific, I'm certain, but it also means a lot of *schlock* too.

Joy is used sometimes in association with peace. Which is another devious word we've got to talk about sometime. But how about the end of letters that are signed "Peace and Joy, Fred."

First of all you've got to check the letterhead to see which Fred the Peace and Joy came from and then the content of the letter is so critical and scathing, not to mention devious, that the joy gets lost in the shuffle.

Then there're the people who use "joy" and really mean "ha-ha." If you aren't laughing or at least smiling, they look at you as if all the joy (meaning "ha-ha") has gone out of your life. Needless to say, joy is not restrained hilarity or a constant state of subdued giddiness that makes half of the world look at you as if you are high most of the time.

Oh, but the most seductive use of the word is when it is uttered in sacred tones. Joy is elevated to a mystical experience which can't be described to anyone. Well, friend, if you can't describe it, why tell me you have whatever it was again.

Joy! A very beautiful word indeed. Maybe it just means that I like getting up in the morning because today has got to be the best day in my life, and there are going to be a lot of experiences that I never had before. Maybe it means that I missed the world while I was sleeping and can hardly wait to get on with it again.

table of objects

Place a number of different items, ranging in size from a pin or paper clip to a poster, on a table. Arrange the objects any way you desire. Cover the entire table with a cloth. At a signal, uncover the table and give the participants an opportunity to examine the items without touching them. Take only a short time for this (2-3 minutes). Cover the table. Participants pair off and tell each other what they saw on the table. Participants will probably not see everything that is there. Have them discuss with each other why, for example, they think that they didn't see the pin or why they saw the pin and not the three-foot poster. Allow about 10 minutes for this conversation.

Line up the participants in pairs:

A	B
A	B
A	B

Have the partners look at each other and reflect on the conversation which just took place. After 2 or 3 minutes of silent looking, the participants will turn around and sit back to back. On a piece of paper write a description of the other person as you recall him. Turn and compare descriptions. What highlights did you miss in observation? What did you see in the silent looking that you didn't see in the conversation? Have the pairs compare the ways they saw a person as opposed to the way we see objects on a table. How do we see persons? How can we better see persons?

doodles

Using 8½ x 11 paper or pieces of newsprint, draw the way you feel right now. Take about 3 minutes. Post the pictures and discuss in groups of two to six.

Using pieces of newsprint, draw a picture which tells how you feel about yourself. Take about 5 minutes. Post and discuss in groups of two to six.

Draw a picture of another person in the group of two to six. Take about 5 minutes. Put all the pictures in the center. Everyone find themselves and discuss.

VARIATIONS: 1. (For groups of up to twelve participants.) Draw separate pictures of two members of the group. Take about 5 minutes. Put all the pictures in the center. Find picture(s) of yourself and discuss.

2. Collages made from clippings from magazines and newspapers can serve the same purpose. If you use this, have all the necessary materials available. Allow more time for completion of the pictures. Collages take about three times as long as drawings.

famous people

Have the participants place the numbers 1, 2, and 3 on the left-hand side of a piece of paper. Ask each question separately and allow time for clarification and answers.

1. What person in history, movies, books, television, or politics do you most closely identify with?

2. What person in history, movies, books, television, or politics do you most dislike?

3. What person in history, movies, books, television, or politics would you most like to be like?

After all of the participants have answered the questions, have them get into groups of two or three and share their answers. Tell your partner(s) why you chose the names you chose. What is there in you that makes you feel the way you do?

first names

For groups of up to twelve. If the group is larger, subdivide into groups of equal size.

Participants stand in a circle. Each participant picks an adjective that starts with the same letter as his first name, e.g., Boisterous Bill. He says his name with the adjective preceding it by way of introducing himself. The person to his left repeats his name with the adjective, then introduces himself in like manner. The person again to the left must do the same, first using the names and adjectives of persons preceding him, then his own. The process continues around the circle. If any person forgets a name, he must go to that person and ask his name before the process can continue. This is a good opener, even though a name tells very little about a person. The interesting part of this exercise for discussion is the descriptive words that persons choose for themselves. You may want to use the experience as an opener. For example, "Bill, of all the available words in the language, why did you choose 'boisterous'?" The names that are chosen are valuable information and help groups to get on and get in faster than the usual coffee hour conversation.

LOOKING BACK

When I first loved
Her
I gave words
Written on clouds
Blown by the
Wind.

coat of arms

PURPOSE: To provide an opportunity for new groups to get to know each other or deepen the understanding that already existing groups have of each other.

MATERIALS NEEDED: Piece of paper and felt-tipped pen or crayon for each participant.

PROCEDURE: 1. Each participant is given a piece of paper and asked to draw the outline of a coat of arms or shield with six separate spaces.

2. Each participant is asked to draw five pictures or symbols in five of the spaces:

    a. What I like to do.

    b. What I do well.

    c. What failure I have experienced in the last six months.

    d. What long-range goal I have for myself.

    e. What I would be willing to die for.

Have the participants draw the pictures or symbols one at a time. Wait until all have completed a picture before going on to the next. When the pictures are completed (10-15 minutes), proceed to the sixth space.

3. In the remaining space, have each participant write three words that he would like on his gravestone which he hopes would describe him.

4. In groups of two to six share the coat of arms. Tell the group about it, what it means, and why you did what you did with it.

VARIATION: Another way to do this is to have the group members comment on the shields and let the individual comment by way of addition to the comments of the rest. In either case, the knowledge each person has of the others in the group will be tremendously enhanced.

influential persons

Models for group participation and leadership roles are determined to a large degree by persons who influence you. To help your group look at those persons who have influenced them, and to begin to discover why these persons were influential, use the following questions:

1. List three persons having considerable influence in your life. Include their names, occupation, and relationship to you.

2. Who has been the most influential person in your life so far? Again, include this person's occupation and relationship to you.

3. List the names, occupation, and relationship of three persons to whom you would turn in time of trouble.

4. What characteristics of these people appeal to you most?

PROCEDURE: 1. Give each person a sheet of 8½ x 11 paper. Ask them each of the above questions. Allow time for participants to answer each question before going to the next.

2. When everyone has answered all the questions, divide into groups of two to six to talk about the questions and the answers each gave. What kinds of persons have been influential in the lives of the group? Are there any common characteristics of these people? Do you look at yourself any differently now that you have looked at those who have influenced you?

Don't try to be me…**be.**

double dialogue

PURPOSE: To discover the role of facts versus feelings in the move toward intimacy.

MATERIALS NEEDED: Sets of dialogue cards with one incomplete sentence on each. Set A deals with facts and Set B deals with feelings. Use Set A for the first part of the exercise and Set B for the second part. Samples of Sets A and B may be found below.

NUMBER OF PARTICIPANTS: Any number of people over four. Preferably an even number, though the exercise can be used with uneven numbers with slight modification.

PROCEDURE: Have the participants pair with someone they do not know. The pairs are not to say anything to each other until the signal is given. Using Set A of the cards, each partner in the pair completes the sentence. He does not go on to the next card until his partner has completed hers. Take turns going first. Do not turn to the next card until each partner has completed his sentence verbally to his partner.

When the process is completed, the pair separates. Each person then finds another person whom they do not know and follows a similar procedure using Set B. Again the partners should not engage in any conversation until they have received Set B of the cards. Do not go on to the next card until the partner has completed his sentence. Take turns going first.

After both sets of cards have been used, discuss the implications with the total group, using such questions as:

1. Which person do you feel closer to, A or B?

2. How important are the facts in getting to know each other?

3. Would you like to go to partner A and do Set B?

4. What kinds of things have we learned from this exercise?

Card Set A (one set for each participant):

1. My name is_____.

2. I work at_____.

3. I am (married, single, etc.)_____.

4. I have_____children.

5. My favorite movie was_____.

6. My favorite singer is_____ .

7. My favorite composer is_____ .

Card Set B (one set for each participant):

1. I like_____ .

2. I am afraid of_____.

3. I am happiest when_____ .

4. I am sad when _____.

5. When I meet strangers, I_____.

6. The thing I most like about myself is

_____.

7. I like people to think of me as_____.

hidden agendas

Every group member has a set of unexpressed agendas affecting the group formation, personal involvement, and future action. To help your group become aware of these "hidden agendas," use the following exercise.

Start a conversation, discussion, or business meeting. After about 10 minutes, stop the group conversation, no matter where they are. Ask each individual to write down on a 3 x 5 card exactly what he was thinking of at that moment, whether it was a thing, person, issue, or problem. You jot down what it was that was actually being said at the moment you stopped the conversation. Have each participant tell what he wrote on the card. Then pick up the conversation where it left off.

Repeat this exercise two additional times.

After you have stopped the conversation three times, discuss the experience. What effect does lack of attention, thinking about something else, outside pressures, and intergroup feeling have on group development and decisions?

MEDITATION

Turn it off, Lord, the Ark isn't finished yet.

We talk about community.
And it's nice.
But the thing that hangs us up is
That we'd like to get
Our own thing together
First.
Then we would look good.
Then we would be beautiful.
But we can't afford that luxury
Anymore.
We gotta go in.
We gotta go in
Just the way we are.

SUMMARY

We all want to
Make certain our boats
Are finished
Before it starts to rain.

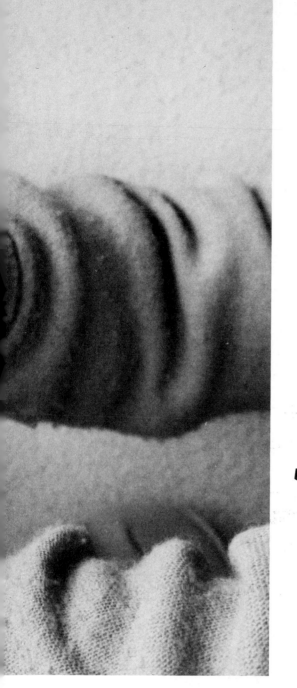

win/lose

Win/Lose is the most expected thing in our culture that two or more people do who get together and are in the process of getting to know each other. Competition is the American Way; well, at least it's the Little League way. Remember all the people you were told about who were failures because they didn't have the drive to get to the top. They didn't take what they could get. They didn't know how to hustle.

Maybe they knew how to hustle and chose not to because they cared about other people too much. One of the reasons we play win/lose is that we don't know how to let people know us too well. We can't let people know we care. That leaves us wide open to get hurt. No one likes getting hurt. If we let people know we care, we are so open that they can reject us. That's why most of us form our own bands. We never have to worry about being asked to play.

The readings, songs, and exercises in this section will help you and your group to first identify the win/lose hump and then take some steps to get over it.

NO HIDING PLACE

Split-level dreams
On half-acre heavens
Invaded by the neighbor kids
Lily white
Up tight
Hiding places.
Twenty thousand plus
Inflation
Taxes
Fireplace in the rec room
Tile on the floor
Wall to wall carpets
Under roof shopping mall
Hiding places

Chorus: But it really doesn't matter
            Just what you do
            'Cause the changes'll roll right over you

Jesus save
My hiding place

Contemporary gothic
Architecturally sound
Open-beamed
Highspired
Wooden altar
Hiding places.
Lily white
Up tight
Pastors
People
Wall to wall
Statement and directive
Hiding places

Chorus: But it doesn't really matter
            Just what you do
            'Cause the changes'll roll right over you

SONG

The whole world is my country.

Flew out of O'Hare
Early one morn
Took the northeast route
To New York City
Looked at Ohio
And those little tiny farms
But

There ain't no
black lines
red lines
green lines
dotted lines
double lines
Drawn on the ground.
It's only our mind
That's put them there.

But . . . there's
food lines
job lines
traffic lines
poor lines
sick lines
And, that ain't our minds
That put them there.
The whole world is my country.

newspaper costume

Inexpensive materials, such as newspapers, rags, magazines, crayons, and masking tape, can be used effectively in creating exercises and simulations which will help groups learn more about themselves, each other, and how it is they work and relate to each other. Here is one which is good for team building.

MATERIALS NEEDED: Newspapers and masking tape.

NUMBER OF PARTICIPANTS: Teams of about five each.

TIME: 1 hour.

TASK: To make a newspaper costume for one team member.

PROCEDURE: Each team is given two or three packets of rolled-up newspaper with a rubber band holding the roll together. They also get a roll of masking tape. Allow 25 minutes of planning time. This is a competitive exercise. The task is to design the most creative costume possible to be worn by one member of the team. During the planning, they may not open the rolls of newspaper. At the end of the planning time they will have an opportunity to make the costume and will be given 7 minutes to do so. Everyone has a chance to look at the other costumes and evaluate them. The leader serves as judge for the best.

PROCESS: Ask questions dealing with the way people work together, such as: Why was the wearer chosen? What could be done to improve the team's effectiveness? What did the competitive feelings do to their effectiveness? How did they feel if their costume was not judged best? If it was judged best?

REPRACTICE: Use similar packets of paper. Only 15 minutes of planning time is permitted, and construction time is cut to 2 minutes. The leader is the judge and again allows for observations to be made by participants.

The repractice allows for observations about change and team building. Did the teams work better the second time? Why? What factors contributed to the second design that were not present in the first? Did the winner of the first use the same design a second time? What changes caused the increased efficiency?

What we see and like, we tend to change to.

VARIATION: Use Tinker Toys exercise as the repractice, or vice versa.

RALPH'S BUNNY DIED

On some Easter morning more years ago than either of them care to remember, the boys got out of bed and ran downstairs to see what the Easter Bunny left for them hidden behind the chairs and radiators.

Bunnies! Real live breathing bunnies in a box on the living room floor. One for Jack and the other for Ralph.

"They both look the same."

"How can we tell them apart?"

"We'll remember."

On some Easter Monday more years ago than either of them care to remember, one of the bunnies died.

"Ralph's bunny died," said Jack.

"Jack's bunny died," said Ralph.

"*A* bunny died," said Mother, and they both cried.

BURNING HOUSES

Burning houses
Draw crowds
As sirens squeal,
Wail,
Signal
The curious
Almost anywhere
To come and celebrate
The dancing, darting flames
Drinking water,
Smoking, belching,
Laughing,
Entertaining
Coffee drinking,
Loudly talking
People.

Change us,
Concern us,
Burn in us
Celebrating.
Draw us to your
Laughing flame.

SONG

WHAT ARE WE GONNA DO?

What are we gonna do
About that birdsong
Coming clearly
Through our window?

What are we gonna do
About the child
Who's almost grown
And gone?

Chorus: Well, the wind just keeps blowin'
And the rain keeps on fallin'
I can't stop clouds from movin'
But I've tried.

Small things don't last forever
They go by so quickly.

What are we gonna do
About the fire
That's burning down
Our home?

What are we gonna do
About the many dreams
We had
So long ago?

What are we gonna do
About the love songs
We never got
To sing?

Chorus: Well, the wind just keeps blowin'
And the rain keeps on fallin'
I can't stop clouds from movin'
But I've tried.

Small things don't last forever
They go by so quickly.

tinker toys

MATERIALS NEEDED: One small set of Tinker Toys for each team of participants. (Another option is to take a large set and divide it equally among the participants. It is important that each team have enough materials to work with.)

NUMBER OF PARTICIPANTS: Divide any number into teams of approximately equal size (three to eight). This exercise does not work well with only one team. A competitive spirit will be engendered when more than one team is working at it. The more teams, the merrier.

TIME: 55 minutes.

TASK: To build the highest possible structure which is self-supporting. Twenty-five minutes will be permitted for planning verbally, and the construction will be done nonverbally in 2 minutes.

PROCEDURE: 1. Each team takes 25 minutes to plan. They can empty the can of Tinker Toys but they may not touch any of the pieces. All the drawing and planning they care to do is permitted. The only stipulation is that they not touch the pieces in the set, or place any pieces together.

2. After the 25 minute planning session, each team places all the pieces back in the can.

3. At a signal, the teams begin. They have 2 minutes to build their structure. During the construction, they may not talk to each other.

4. The leader of the event signals the time. After the 2 minutes, he calls time. Let the groups vent their feelings. It will take a little while for groups to calm down and complete their "oh's" and "ah's." Do not make any judgments about the best one. Let the participants make such remarks informally.

LEARNING FROM THE EXPERIENCE: Several questions will help your group to learn about themselves, how they work with each other, and what spirit they had in the approach to the task. You are interested in the open kinds of comments that this exercise will engender. The following may serve as a starter for you:

1. How did your team do?

2. Did each member of your team participate in the task? Did each team member understand the task? Did some sit back and watch? What did this do to the team effort?

3. Was the final plan for the structure one person's suggestion or did the whole team contribute in the planning effort?

4. Did your team have an observable leader? Did someone tend to dominate? What did it do to the total effort of the team?

5. Did your team feel as if you were in competition with the other teams? Where did this feeling come from? Refer to the phrasing of the task: to build the highest possible structure which is self-supporting. No one said anything about competition. Where do you think we get these ideas?

6. What does this exercise say about the way groups plan? Areas to consider: working together on a task, importance of the involvement of all participants, leadership, ratio of planning time to doing time.

USES: Any group that is coming together for the first time to plan a specific event or course of action will find this helpful for identifying the factors which make planning difficult, and those factors which help effective planning.

Groups that have had difficulties in planning and executing courses of action will find this helpful in identifying the factors which may be getting in the way of effective action. All the participants are not with it; not everyone understands what it is they are trying to do.

Highly competitive groups will discover that competition is both a positive and negative factor in doing the job. Some teams may see that competition with other teams hindered their own effective performance.

VARIATIONS: 1. Some planning efforts require the coordination of two separate groups. Two committees or two organizations are working together on a common problem and need to come out at the point of action about the same time. Competition is a real factor here, as is the difficulty of coordination.

Do the same exercise with pairs of teams. Allow 15 minutes of planning in separate teams. Take 5 minutes to let the team pairs coordinate their efforts, and allow a final 10 minutes of planning the joint effort in individual teams.

Allow 3 minutes for the construction of the joint effort. Again the no talking rule applies for the construction, as well as placing the pieces in the can prior to the construction. The task is the same.

Similar questions may be used to discover some things about working together. You may wish to concentrate some of the questions in the area of joint planning. What happened after the two groups talked together? Were original plans changed? Did the joint structure fit together well? What happens when attempts to coordinate efforts are made? How can two groups plan together more effectively?

2. BUILD AN ANIMAL. This exercise uses the same materials and teams as the above Tinker Toy exercise, and many of the same learnings may be drawn from it. The basic learning is how effectively each group functioned as a team.

TASK: To build an animal nonverbally.

PROCEDURE: 1. The leader explains the task to the teams. Each team is to build an animal nonverbally. They are to proceed immediately with the task, with no prior discussion, even as to the kind of animal they will be building. Allow 10 minutes for them to complete the animal.

2. Talk about the experience. Questions you might consider may be found above, under LEARNING FROM THE EXPERIENCE.

3. Repeat the exercise, allowing 5 minutes for building the animal.

4. Talk about the repractice. Did each team function together better in the repractice? What made the difference?

Single track minded
People
Find it hard
To understand
What an up down
Turned around
Many directed man
Is all about.

But then
So do the many directed
People
Find it hard
To understand
Each other
'Cause they change so
Fast and often
Never stepping
In the same waterway
More than once.

They wonder
If the other man's the same
And find it easiest
To assume
That
The world stands still
While they are drifting by.

squares

Nonverbal tasks can be used to test communication skills and leadership potential of those participating in the task. In the following exercise, full cooperation and a win/win mind-set are necessary for proper completion of the task. If your group is still at the win/lose stage of interaction, this exercise can be a valuable tool to get at the destructiveness of this way of thinking and acting.

Six members of the group will be involved in the task itself; the rest of the group will act as observers and will participate with the six in the discussion at the end of the exercise.

PROCEDURE: 1. Cut five squares as shown:

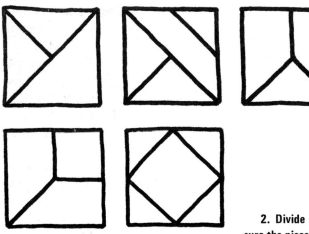

2. Divide the pieces into six piles. Make sure the pieces are thoroughly mixed up.

3. Select six individuals and give them the following instructions: (a) Construct squares of equal size; (b) you can only *give* a piece to another; (c) you cannot *take* a piece from another person's pile; (d) the whole task is done nonverbally. Allow the six to work for 15 minutes.

4. At the end of 15 minutes, talk about the experience. How does communication take place without words? What leadership roles emerged? Did any one person complete his square at the expense of another? How was full cooperation necessary to the completion of the task? If the task was not completed, why wasn't it?

To All the Parents Using Their Children

If they only knew
How scared he was
And how much he hated it
They'd never say
He had a lovely voice.

BUTTONS AND BUMPER STICKERS

If only people who need
Had the courtesy
To wear big buttons
Saying "Least of These"
Or "Jesus"
Or anything
To remind us
Of the truth.

SONG

GOOD IDEAS

The grasshopper hopped to the frog's front door,
He said I've got no food in store
And the winter is acomin' on fast.
Do you have enough for both to last
Us through.

Mr. Frog "come in" and sit yourself down.
You clearly got a problem we should talk around.
I'll cogitate and meditate and think it all out.
We'll find an answer. All I'll do is think about
The cold.

Chorus:

Good ideas don't make it
By themselves.
It takes a lot of livin'
To make the dream come true.
Thinking by itself
Won't see us through.

.Hopper.

Frogs by their nature can sleep the winter through.
Hibernation is your answer. You'll keep from turnin' blue.
There's an answer to the problem of the winter food crisis.
Turn into a frog, before you turn to ice. Is
That a help.

Thanks frog.

Chorus:

Sittin' in the church on the Sunday morn
The man was tryin' to tell me just why I was born
To serve my fellowman his big voice boomed
And the church was filled with people well groomed . . .
Thinking nice.

Thanks frog.

Chorus:

Now here is all we need to do, to make the world better
For children and their friends. Black, white, yellow, red.
We gotta love one another and get our thing together.
What a beautiful answer. Love and get together
Right now.

Thanks frog.

Chorus:

Now frogs have the answer to all us hoppers freezin'
In the cold. We gotta find the secret ways to keep from sneezin'.
We'll love, and sing, and dance . . . and get our thing together.
All we gotta do, is turn into a frog. Never mind the weather
Or my achin' stomach.

Thanks frog.

Chorus:

tribulation road

This is a nonverbal simulation usable for learning about group cooperation. The fine details are up to you, the leader. It is recommended for groups of twelve to fifteen (although more may be possible). The outline for the simulation is as follows:

The group is going on an imaginary journey. Directions for the trip are provided and should be written in imaginary terms using the physical setting of your meeting or retreat as the basis. At four or five points along the way, the group will encounter some trials and tribulations that you have written and posted in advance. No matter what story you devise at each location, the result is the blinding or crippling of some of the group members. A ratio of two blind persons to one crippled person is required. It is never stated who has received these inflictions; that is a group decision which must be made nonverbally. The criteria for the journey are: (a) the simulation is totally nonverbal; (b) the group must stay together the whole time; and (c) if you are assigned or take an infliction, you must play it out. If complete cooperation emerges, the journey will be completed. If not, you still will have some exciting feelings to work with and learnings about the nature of responsibility and cooperation.

Spread the accidents over the course of the journey. By the last accident, all the participants should be afflicted in some manner.

WHAT'S LEFT OF THE APPLE TREE

Two feet of ugly stump
About ten scruffy bent shoots
Surrounding it
Some older than the others
So little left
That even the birds
Forgot
They used to sit and sing on
Its branches.

I first saw it in the winter
When trees like that
Are even uglier
Than when covered by a few
Leaves hiding
Weeds and dead things
Around the stump.

We'll cut it down in the spring
And give the grass a chance.

Came the spring
The daffodils grew
Dotting the lawn with
Splashes of yellow
And white
The tulips
Red and white and orange
Maple leaves bright green
Pear trees blossoming
And unnoticed because of the
Others
Several delicate blossoms
On an ugly branch
Of what was left of the apple tree.

Came the summer
Rich green
Summer flowers
Children swinging
Dogs digging the new planted places
Warm sun
Patting my head
As I push the rotary around
Making the lawn
As much like an estate as the weeds
Would allow
And tiny green balls began to form
On what was left of the apple tree.

The pears grew abundantly
We looked around among
Our acquaintances
Trying to find
Anyone who liked them
Pearsauce
Pearbutter
Pear pie
Pear brown betty
Ridiculous.
Do you know how few people like pears?

The small green balls were bigger now
Began to take final shape
Large and green
With cheeks beginning to flush
Red
Apples

Lord,
Why so many pears
And so few apples?

break out!

After groups have been formed using one of several procedures, have each group stand in a circle and hold hands. One of their number stands in the middle. His task is to try to break out. The task of the group is to get him to stay. This is a very intense experience and needs to be talked about after it is completed. Many feelings are generated by the experience and need to be handled. Make it clear at the beginning that this experience is a physical expression of unity. The group wants to keep in all of its members.

Should the man in the middle break out, his task becomes that of getting into another group. The group task is to keep its member in and the other's out.

Set a time limit of about 5-10 minutes. When the time has elapsed, sit back and relax. Talk about the feelings generated. What can we say about belonging and not belonging? What is it like to try to stay together? This kind of intense play is a valid team builder.

CONFESSION

I do not need
Reminding
Of murders
And thievery
Committed
By my hand.

I do not need
Reminding
Of hatreds
And hurtings
Committed
By my hand.

They are always with me.

I do not need
Reminding
Of my Lord.

I remember it all
So well.
It is
Always with me.

Like him.

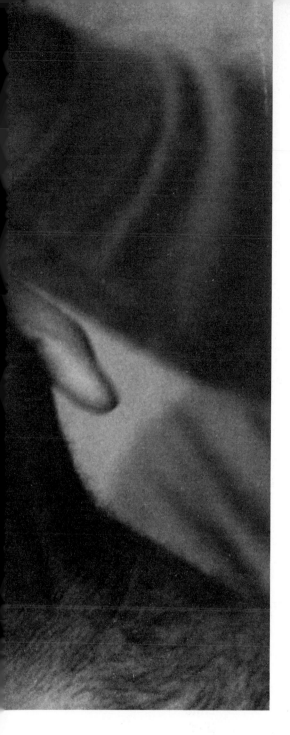

lose/lose

If I can't get what I want, I'm going to make sure you don't get what you want, either.

and to all a good night

a toast to all
the mothers protecting
their children
and the fathers
fighting for
their homes
peace
and quiet
santa will bring
the christ
child

only minutes
before
her body was
lying
atop two small
ones
the younger
sucking at her
breast
the lifeblood
that results
in manhood
and dreams

to all the mothers
drink
the sorrow
the tears
peace
brought
the christ
child
lying on the road
under her

my lai
why cry
santa claus
will never die
color pictures
bloody red
drink it down
and go to bed
peace
quiet
christ
the child

men were meant to die
women for doing the baby thing
children for playing
pets for taking care of
sharing the life together
orderly

he tried to reach the water
for cooling
his parched
dry throat
baked in the sun
hot humid
lips touched
the pool
he
died
crucified
by roman legions

jolly old st nicholas
lend an ear to me
shoot the plastic soldiers
underneath the tree
fake it general custer
sitting bull is gone

to all the mothers
of christ
and brothers
and fathers
child
peace
but never quiet

only wanted
to play in the woods
watch the animals
jump in the grass
roll in the fall leaves
celebrate the sun
child
died
at the hands of
don't walk on the grass signs

tag them all
drink
to another world
peace
chrïst child
quiet
later

dream

I dreamed it was
the last day of my life and
everyone I met talked about tomorrow.

ROLE PLAY

I was sheriff once. It was only for a little while, a couple of hours, in a make-believe town. We all knew who everyone else was because of the tags we wore.

The situation . . . like a real town with streets and shops and banks and even churches. No town is complete without churches though sometimes you wonder why they are there. As a matter of fact, you wonder why other things are there too.

But I was the sheriff, though only for a little while. And the man that lurked inside wanted to be the boss. It would only take a little manipulating to take it all over. Just like "Gunsmoke." I would be more than the sheriff, responsible to no one, looking like I cared for everyone.

But the mayor and the judge ganged up on me. They wanted things to work right. They wanted problems to be resolved. But . . . if all the problems went away, they wouldn't need a sheriff anymore.

If I can't be boss, you won't be either. Set up impossible laws and 30-second parking meters. Stop signs in the middle of the block. No smoking anywhere signs. Make it a law that walking on the sidewalk is illegal and so is walking on the streets.

I was sheriff once. It was only for a while in a make-believe town. I couldn't be in charge and I felt very small for a long time afterwards. They wouldn't let me in. I was a sheriff who didn't matter. Things were taken care of without me.

SONG

Je-sus,
You were lucky!

Jesus,
You were blessed.
Crying only once in a while.
Climbing only one hill.
Carrying only one cross.
One trip up,
Death,
And peace.

Chorus: Jesus,
What a lucky man you were,
Being killed at thirty-three.
Jesus,
Why were so many years
Thrust
Down on me?

Je-sus,
You were lucky!

Jesus,
You were blessed.
You knew
Where peace
Was
And future tomorrows.
I don't even
Know what
This afternoon
Will bring.

Chorus:

life-styles

Have a wide selection of magazines and newspapers available in your meeting room. Participants take about **15** minutes to find photographs or news stories which depict a variety of different life-styles. Of the ones selected, the participants identify one which particularly repulses them (one which they would like to destroy) and one which particularly appeals to them (one which they would like to be a part of). Divide into groups of two or three and discuss why you chose the ones you did. Why do participants want to be like one life-style and not another? What are the appealing factors in choosing a life-pattern?

THE MACHINE'S GOT HOLD OF YOU

The machine has a life of its own
Because it breathes
And vomits
Products
Never as good as you wanted
Them to be
But they're done
No turning back
To see the past
Just plug in every morning
Unplug at the end of the day
Get a couple of belts
And pray that you don't get
Liver trouble.

No one ever makes a mistake
It's the machine that's wrong
But we built
The monster
Eating men alive
Recharging corpses
Breathing life
Into tired people
Pushing the spring
Schedule
Needs to be finished before
The summer
Fall winter spring
Summer
Fall
But you never fall
Always move forward
For mankind
And slam another door in the face
Of someone who's not too bad.

You slam the door in someone's face
Who's not too bad
Basically.
There's no time to talk
Even if you wanted to
But you don't.
Just pound away
Making forward progress
To the end
Of the job
To be met by another
Bigger
Challenge
Give me rest
It's eating me alive.

" . . . the grantee must be a person, either
natural or artificial, in existence at
the time of the conveyance and capable
of taking title." So reads the ruling
ending the legal battle which
resolved that God has no property
rights in the State of California.

MONOPOLY

Monopoly isn't fun anymore. I can remember getting together for a pleasant evening. Talking quickly and drinking beer.

"Hurry up. Get the board."

Far into the night, negotiating, building houses, going into hock for hotels. Saying mock prayers that *they* land on Boardwalk with its hotel. That'll kill them. Even a railroad would be OK because you own them all.

"$23.00 rent."

We all laughed at the absurdly low figure. Nothing compared to the thousands you stand to make if someone lands on Boardwalk.

Then you get a Chance Card which takes you past GO, and $200.00. They are angry and perhaps a little anxious about the possibility of landing on Boardwalk.

"2:00 A.M. already. The babysitter's mother will be furious. We told her about midnight."

"Wait! Don't touch the money."

We'll keep a record of who has what for the next pleasant get-together. Headaches and frustration because we tried to wipe each other out.

It's only a game.

on the pole

For groups of twelve or less.

When played by a group of trusting persons, this exercise can be a great physical relief and source of learnings. Get a pole about eight to ten feet long. A wooden clothes pole or a 1½-2″ diameter pole will do. Lay it on the floor or the grass in the middle of the group, which stands in a circle around it. The instructions are to do with the pole whatever you want. As many can become involved as care to. The only rule is play fairly and carefully. The pole exercise will reveal such things as the subgroups which have formed and the individuals who are asserting themselves. Before the Control and Intimacy questions have been faced and dealt with, it is likely that a lot of counterforce of the Win/Lose, Lose/Lose variety will appear. Do not use this exercise if you are not trained or prepared to deal with conflict. You may do more harm than good. After intimacy has been reached, the pole is a good device to use as an instrument of play.

You may want to follow play on the pole with a free-form group dance, touching hands only. Stand in a circle and touch the tips of fingers rather than holding hands. Move in any manner that the group chooses.

WHEELS ON THE ALTAR

My God, My God
Why have you been carved
From a block of marble
Way up front
Where I have to strain to see you
Let alone understand
What's going on.

You think
If I put roller skates
Under the corners
We could move you
Out
Where you belong.

Yes!
Roll you right down the street
Like a fancy
Soapbox derby car
Clacking along
Past the shoe repair man
The barber and the appliance dealer
Wheel you on down
Right to my house.

You could live there
If you wanted
Got an extra room for special guests
Even has electricity
To plug in a lamp
So you could read
Late at night
And we'll call you in the morning
When the coffee's ready.

But that's another dumb thought
Like Jesus.
Nobody listened
Unless he fed them and healed
Or did a magic trick
Like raising dead people
And stuff like that.

We can't afford to put wheels
On the altar
Ego boosted architects
Would starve
And there'd be no one to
Read the pamphlets
On the good deeds
The money's done behind your back.

Guess you're stuck
Right where you are
Way up front
Getting dusty
Being pampered
We really put you in your place.

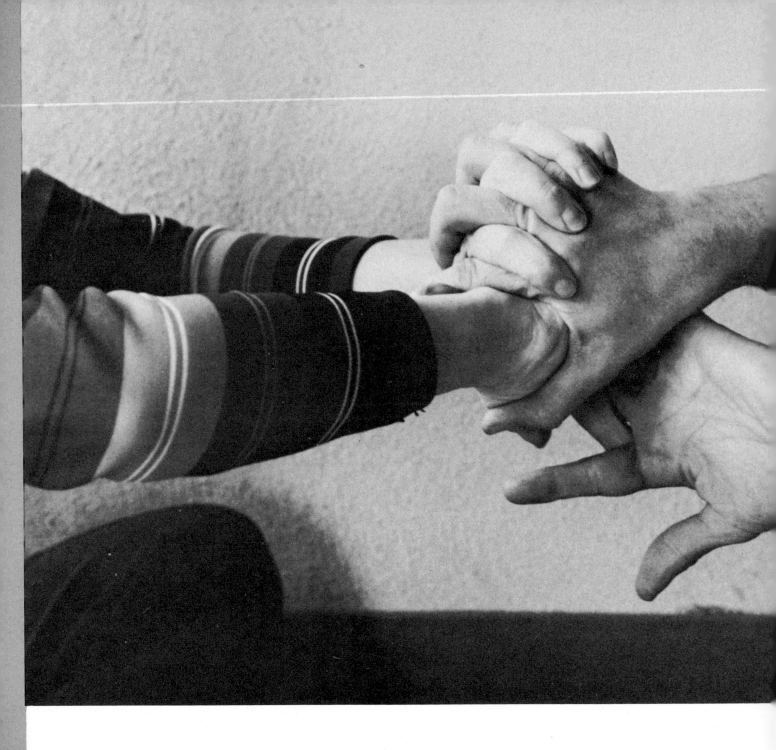

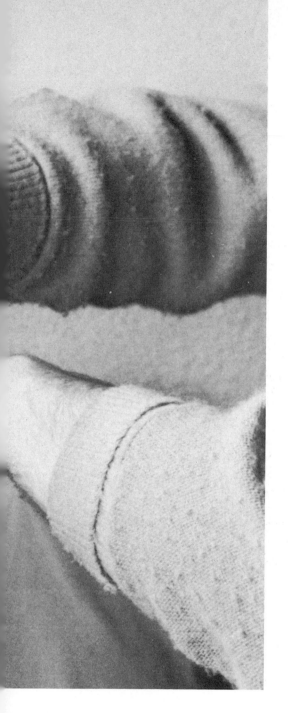

control

There is no way that two or more can play together until the Control questions have been met head on. Who's in charge? Why do you need to be in charge? Don't you trust us? Who do you want us to think you are? Why is that important to you?

This is the most difficult of all moves as people begin to know each other. Reminiscences of earlier "play" creep in. It all seemed so great, but here we are and we don't know what to do next. We're frustrated. There are crazy fears creeping around our heads and bodies. Why couldn't we just go back and pretend that everything was fine? Don't pry too deeply. Leave other people alone. That's the kind of thing we've been taught.

Well, here we are. We've identified the fact that it is easy for us to play Win/Lose and Lose/Lose. We don't like that a bit. It might be comfortable somewhere, but not here. We want to move on. But what are we getting into? What am I afraid of? I trust every one of you, don't I?

No! I don't. I want to but I don't. You don't either. I was afraid that I was the only one who. . . .

Now you're on the way. Hang in. We're on the way.

where am I?

Small groups of twelve or less who have had some time together can use this exercise to visualize their progress. Stand in a circle. Take 2 minutes in silence in which the participants will pick a place to stand which they feel best illustrates their position in relation to the rest of the group. Do they feel close to one person? Do they feel as if they are really not part of the group? Are they close to a few members but separated from the rest?

At a signal, have them move to the place they have chosen and sit down. Discuss the positions as openly as possible. As the discussion proceeds, members may change their positions. For example, a member who felt that the group had been ignoring him may learn that his observations were inaccurate.

VARIATION: Have the group stand in a circle. Elect one member to move the participants to the positions he thinks best represents where they are in relation to the group. When completed, sit down and discuss as above.

When you want to be in charge and finally make it, there's no fun anymore. The fun is in the getting there. That's old stuff, I know. But if the fun is in the getting there, then there must be a way of always getting there with no concern about whether you make it or not. The joy is in the struggle, not the fighting.

hands Have the group members pair off. Each pair sits facing each other, close together. Clasp hands with your partner. Close your eyes. Touching only your partner's hands, express the following: (The leader calls out each phrase. Allow about 50-60 seconds for each one.)

1. Greet each other.

2. Play together.

3. Struggle (have a conflict).

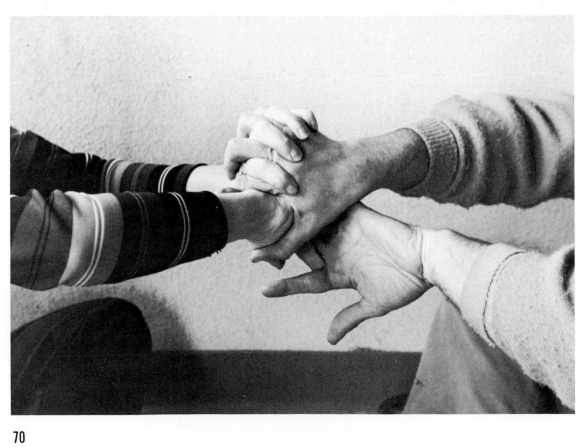

4. Resolve the conflict.

5. Hold and support each other.

6. Play again.

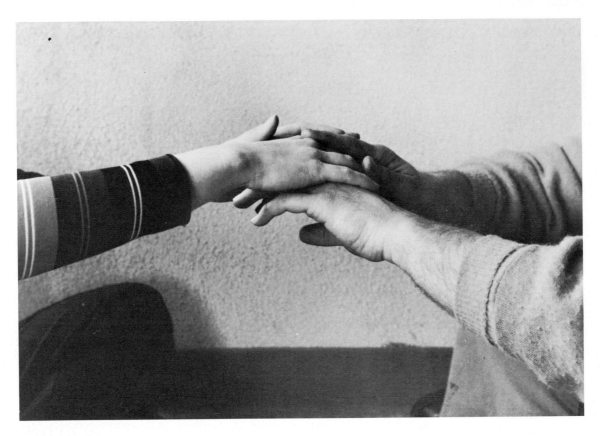

7. Say good-bye.

At the end of this exercise, have the pairs talk together about the experience. Which part did they like? Why? Which part did they dislike? Why? What did they learn about the other person? This is an excellent exercise for couples.

VARIATION: In groups of two or three, touching hands only, go through a nonverbal liturgy:

1. Invocation — greeting.
2. Play — dance.
3. Hymn — sing.
4. Gospel/Sermon.
5. Prayer desires.
6. Benediction — say good-bye.

There are **no limits**

'til someone tells you
you've gone too far

even then
they could
well be
wrong *!*

circle of community

Stand in a circle. Not too close to each other, only close enough so that if you stretched out your arms you could touch another person's hand. Stand in a circle so that you can see all other members of the group. Relax and close your eyes. Look deeply into yourself. What do you see inside yourself? How do you feel? Are you happy? Do you feel conspicuous? Are you sad? Are you embarrassed by not being able to see everyone else? Do you like what you see inside yourself? Look around your mind. Are there things that you can see that no one else knows? Are there happy things that you can recall that make you want to smile? What you see inside yourself is you. No one else knows you as completely as you do. Keep your eyes closed. Now bring your hands up in front of you, palms facing you. Don't open your eyes. Now open your eyes and look at your hands. Just look at your own hands. Don't look at anyone else. Look at their shape. Do they have long fingers or short fingers? Are they old hands or young hands? Are they hard, calloused hands or soft hands? These hands are different from everyone else's. The fingerprints are unique. No one who has ever lived had hands exactly like yours. Your hands are an extension of yourself. Where have they left their marks? What have your hands done? They have loved, they have struck down. They have worked. They have wasted. Your hands have done things that no others have done. Your hands are you. What they do and what they do not do reveal what you are. Your hands are you. Your hands can reach out to one another. Reach out now and join hands. Hold the hands that you touch tightly. Do not look at one another. Just hold hands tightly. Now look around at each member of the group in silence. These hands holding each other are the hands of man reaching out, reaching to each other. May these hands love more than strike down, heal more than hurt, forgive and be forgiven. You are a child of God and the universe. You belong to each other. Let go when you want to.

WHEN THE TV BROKE

Tragedy of tragedies
The picture faded
Right in the middle
Of an old war movie.
Sure
We knew how it would end
Saw it before
And a hundred like it
But the silence
In the family room
Was oppressive.
What do we do now?

She'd read the paper
I ate too much
And sat immobilized
At the opposite end of the sofa.
The kids
Asleep
The dogs
Lying quietly on the floor
One lifted its sleepy head
To look around the room
The silence
Was new to him, too.

How were the kids today?
OK.

How was work today?
OK.

I folded my hands on my lap
She fumbled with the paper.
What do we do now?
How 'bout we try talking
To each other
Really talking?

Didn't have the courage to
Call
The repairman for
Two months
How the kids suffered
Playing with mom and dad
Talking about life and things
Pixies and kings
Strawberry pie
And love.

rooms

This exercise may help married couples or any other couple seeking intimacy to move in the direction of more effective communication. Pairing is important in this exercise, so pair before you begin. The individuals do not work with their partner at first, but will work individually.

On a piece of 8½ x 11 paper draw the basic floor plan of a six-room house. It can be any kind the individual desires—one-story, two-story, townhouse, round—whatever is the preference of the person making the drawing. Allow several minutes for the basic floor plan to be completed.

Have the individuals number the rooms from one to six. The order of importance is not a question here. Therefore, room one may not be the most important room to the individual.

Each will be drawing a picture or symbol in rooms one to five. Describe the items to be depicted one at a time and be certain that all have completed their drawing before going on to the next.

Room #1: Draw or depict the one thing which is your best contribution or what you contribute most to the relationship between you and your partner.

Room #2: Draw or depict the most significant event in the relationship in the past year.

Room #3: Draw or depict the thing that you value most in the relationship.

Room #4: Draw or depict the worst or biggest disappointment in the past year.

Room #5: Draw or depict the one thing you wish for most in this relationship.

In the room numbered six, you will be writing three words.

Room #6: Write three words that to you characterize the relationship at its very best.

After this portion of the exercise is completed, ask the participants whether they feel their drawing needs an extra room. If so, have them draw it and describe its function on the drawing.

When enough time has been allowed to add an extra room, have the pairs share their results. Give plenty of time for adequate sharing.

If more than one pair is doing this in a larger group, allow time for the total group to share what they have learned from the experience. What were the most significant things that came from the exercise?

Meeting you has *torn* me open
To feel everything again.

primary/secondary feelings

The open expression of feelings is crucial to effective communication between two persons. But these feelings must be the basic, primary feelings, not the cover-up, secondary feelings. Primary feelings are those that are "I"-directed; secondary feelings are those that are "you"-directed. For example, primary feelings emerge when you say, "I feel _____," or "When you do _____, I feel _____." Secondary feelings are those that appear in "You are _____" statements. Below are lists of primary and secondary feelings. These lists are by no means exhaustive, but may serve to help you identify the difference between these two kinds of feelings, and to recognize each when you attempt to communicate to another what it is you are feeling.

PRIMARY FEELINGS	SECONDARY FEELINGS
Joyfulness	Hostility
Sexual	Defensiveness
Anger	Sarcasm
Tenderness	Bitterness
Embarrassment	Braggadocio
Guilt	Condescension
Anxiety	
Fear	
Excitement	

It is the communication of primary feelings with which this exercise deals. It is particularly useful with married couples, but can be used with any pair that wishes to enhance their communication.

MATERIALS NEEDED: Four small slips of paper, a pencil, and one 8½ x 11 piece of paper for each participant. List of primary and secondary feelings posted where all can see it.

NUMBER OF PARTICIPANTS: Any number of pairs.

PROCEDURE: 1. First discuss the difference between primary and secondary feelings, as explained above.

2. Have the couples sit back to back. They will be working with the four small slips of paper at this point. On each slip of paper they will be writing a primary feeling or phrase to denote a primary feeling in answer to a question. Allow time for all to answer each question before going on to the next. The four questions are:

a. Think of the most exciting event or occurrence in your entire life. What was the primary feeling you had then? Write it down.

b. Think of the most horrible, traumatic, miserable event or happening in your whole life. What was the primary feeling you had then?

c. What is the primary feeling you most like to experience?

d. What is the primary feeling you least like to experience?

3. Pick one of the experiences and feelings which you would be willing to tell your partner more about than you ever have before. It can be a pleasant or an unpleasant experience. When you have selected one, pass it over your shoulder to your partner. Don't turn around. Read the paper that has been passed to you.

4. After a moment or two, have the participants turn around and begin to tell their partner more about the experience they noted or feeling than they ever had before. Allow 15-20 minutes for this.

5. At the end of the conversation, have the partners sit back to back once again. Think about the conversation you just had with your partner. On the large piece of paper, write a note to your partner telling him or her what that conversation meant to you. When you have finished, pass it over your shoulder to your partner. Read the note that has been passed to you.

6. Turn around and talk to your partner about the note and the total experience. Allow about 10-15 minutes for this.

7. At the end of this conversation, have the pairs re-form as a total group and share their feelings about the experience.

RESPONSIVE READING

One: I value our relationship and want to keep it.
The Other: But I am my own person. I have needs and the right to try to meet them.
One: I will try to treat you as yourself when you are trying to meet your needs or are having problems meeting them.
The Other: I will try to do the same for you. I will try to listen with acceptance and understanding. I will try to help you find your own solutions rather than have you depend on mine.
One: At those times, I will try to modify my behavior for the good of both of us.
The Other: When your behavior interferes with my needs, I will tell you as openly and honestly as I can. I will tell you what it is I'm feeling and trust you will listen and respond.
One: I will respond with openness and integrity. Let us resolve to meet our conflicts with the same openness with which we meet our joys. Let us not push and hold each other down with words or actions.
The Other: I will commit myself to this, so that our relationship can grow and meet our mutual needs as well as our individual ones.
One: Let us continue to relate without fear of losing. Let me never seek to be in charge. Let us be together.
The Other: Let us grow together in love and peace.

intimacy

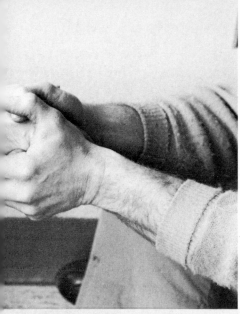

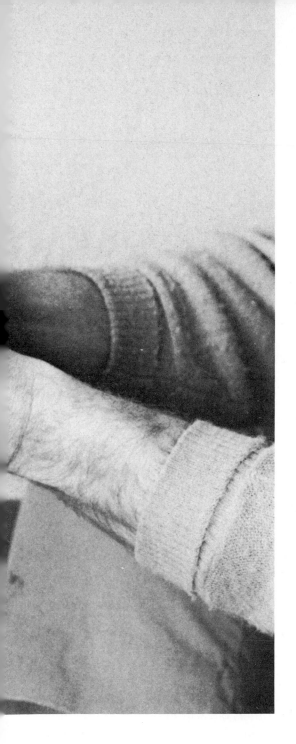

win/win

WIN/WIN

I guess we all know there is more than winning at someone else's expense. I guess we all know that keeping others from getting what they want because they refuse to give us what we want can be equally devastating. I guess we all know it in our heads. Just in our heads, where the information is easily retrievable for dropping in the right settings to make us look good.

It's scary to reach out unafraid of losing or getting hurt when you've been conditioned to take what you can get and run.

We paired off and stood face to face. The instructions were to put your partner down. Use all your strength and put him down. Press hard with everything you have and push him to the floor regardless of the cost of energy or feeling.

He resisted with a lot of force and then through my fingers, I felt the strength going out of the struggle. He was being pushed down to the floor. My strength increased. The first sensation was good. I won. I won. I beat him.

Then the awful hollow feeling.

We changed roles and he tried to put me down. I resisted for the longest time. Tempted to just let him do it. Then I would win. If I didn't really resist, I won because I let him do it. Like the many times you give yourself or something you like to someone else, and then feel that you won because you're such a nice guy. But he put me down for real. I felt rotten and defeated.

We sat together on the floor panting and staring silently. Recitations of our history and the people we have put down came flowing out. Never felt good really. By the time you've won you're alone and nothing is left but dead bodies lying around.

Idea!

Instead of putting down let's try to lift each other up. Sounds impossible but let's try. We sat next to each other, our legs in opposite directions and our hips touching. We gripped each other's arms.

NOW! Everything we had went to the other. All the strength to lift up the other. It will never work. But. . . . It was working. I was being lifted up and not helping myself at all.

Win/Win is real! Use all your strength to lift up and hold up the other, trusting they are doing the same. It's not in my head anymore. Get it out of yours and put it where you live.

SONG

They sit on folding chairs
Against the wall
Silently.
The music is playing
And no one is dancing
People are dying
And no one is crying.

Chorus: Take my hand
Look at the sky.
Watch the young birds
Trying to fly.

Make good-byes
Once
And forever
Meet the
Warm new faces
Smiling walking
Toward the new sun.

Chorus: Take my hand
Look at the sky.
Watch the young birds
Trying to fly.

It's the same
"What kind of people
Live here" question
Never changing.
Music.
No dancing.
Dying.
No crying.

Chorus: Take my hand
Look at the sky.
Watch the young birds
Trying to fly.

build a bridge

This exercise concentrates on the joint effort of two teams. It is helpful in achieving learnings similar to those of the Tinker Toy exercise.

MATERIALS NEEDED: One small set of Tinker Toys for each pair of teams. In addition the leader may choose to make multicolored pipe cleaners available to the pairs. Card tables, one for each team.

NUMBER OF PARTICIPANTS: An equal number of teams, each team having three to eight members. After teams are formed, each team will pair with another team for the exercise.

TIME: 1 hour.

TASK: To have each pair of teams build the most creative and beautiful bridge possible. Each team works on separate ends of the bridge; the completed ends must meet in the middle.

PROCEDURE (for each pair of teams): 1. Divide the Tinker Toys and pipe cleaners, if used, in half, and place each half on a card table. The card tables should be approximately four feet apart.

2. Allow 25 minutes of planning time, during which team members may talk to each other. The two teams, however, may not communicate directly with each other. Choose a separate room away from the main room. Each team selects a negotiator who meets with the other team's negotiator in the separate room. Here is where the final plan emerges. When a negotiator returns it is important that he not relay instructions to his team so loudly that the other team can overhear. No pieces can be put together during the planning time.

3. At the end of the planning time, the pieces are placed in the can.

4. At the signal the teams have 3 minutes to build the bridge without talking.

LEARNING FROM THE EXPERIENCE: For questions which may serve as starters for your group, refer to the Tinker Toy exercise which appears on page 42 of this book. The Bridge is simply another way to gain insights into the complications of planning and action. The highlight of this exercise is that competition between groups gets in the way of completing the larger task, namely, to build a beautiful bridge together.

BLESSED THE CHICKEN HOUSE

I

We started early in the morning
Burning brush
Piled higher
Than it should have been
Being afraid of the gust
Of cold wind
That would take the spark
Flying high
To fire the leaves
Or the trees
Or the neighbor's house.

By now the flame
Settles quietly
The hot coals
Ready to take and eat
Anything you cared to feed them.
Dry brittle boards
Dead branches
And even the giant log
Which took two to carry
We thought it'd never burn
Was gone in an hour.

The old brooder house looked like any moderate wind would blow it over. Like the shacks you see along the road and complain about negligent owners who ought to have more pride than that. "Stand back, it's gonna go this time!" You grab the brittle beam and pull. Take the bar and pry, hear a creak or two, run back a few feet with images of crumbling buildings in your head . . . and nothing. "It didn't fall. But there's nothing holding it up."

GOD MUST'VE

We fed the fire pieces
Stripped from her side
For six hours
Till the darkness
Moved us into the house
Like primitive man
We wondered about
Unknown quantities
And the chicken house that wouldn't fall.

That old shack took a beating
None of us could survive
The game called
Onacounta darkness
Chicken house one
Men nothing.
Maybe that was a final.

II

Let me tell you
People
That you only thought
You knew
But now I'm here
I'll tell you
All there is to know
Like change is what
We really need.

The foundations are crumbling
Right under you
Committees are passé
"Groupy" is the thing
And all we have to do
Is wish a tiny wind
To blow it all down.
"Stand back,
It's gonna go this time."

Half the foundation's gone
To hell in the basement
Next to the boiler
Right under the altar
We took the supporting beams
"It didn't fall
But there's nothing holding it up!"

God must've blessed
More than the chicken house.

I am what I am.

That's enough for a start.

You are what you are.

That's enough for both of us.

HE IS BORN! HOORAY!

He is Born!
Hooray!
And with us
Giving peace
To all men
But most especially
You
And me.

He has come
To worlds unseen
Giving peace
In unknown other names
But most especially
You
And me.

His chosen people
None outside
Recognize
Its presence
Whatever called
But most especially
You
And me.

mirror game (outdoors)

This is a good outdoor exercise for maintaining contact with each other. Each person has a pocket mirror. There are no specific instructions except that the person who is designated leader gets the sun's rays and the participants pass it around. Take turns being the leader and be as creative as possible in passing the light around. Try to maintain light contact at all times.

stiff legs/stiff arms

This is another cooperation simulation that will help to learn some things about the feelings which accompany cooperation. Participants pair off. Each pair sits on the floor together. Remove shoes and socks. By a decision within the pair, one partner is stiff-legged and the other stiff-armed. The task of the pair is to put on their shoes and socks. It can be done.

VARIATIONS: 1. Select a volunteer pair and place them in the center with the rest of the group around them. The task of the pair is the same as above. Do not tell the rest of the group that they may not participate. If any member tries to help, it will only speed the process and result in some valid "Good Samaritan" type learnings. Group members might hinder the task as well as help, which is a valid learning for "helpful" people.

2. The pairs have the task of lifting each other up. The only way a pair in this condition (stiff legs/stiff arms) can get up is with a complete win/win mind-set.

The one thing that a dreamer
Need never fear
Is having the dream come true.

By the time this happens
A new dream
Has replaced it.

SONG

Dreamers
Never need to worry
That their dreams
Will all come true.
Others
New and grander
Will always take their place.

Peace is a thing for now.
Quiet a dream for tomorrow.
There is God.
There is Jesus.
Not much else really matters
Not quiet
Or equity
Or retirement
Or mortgage payments
Or other treasures
That holy men don't need.

Thank you for letting me be me.

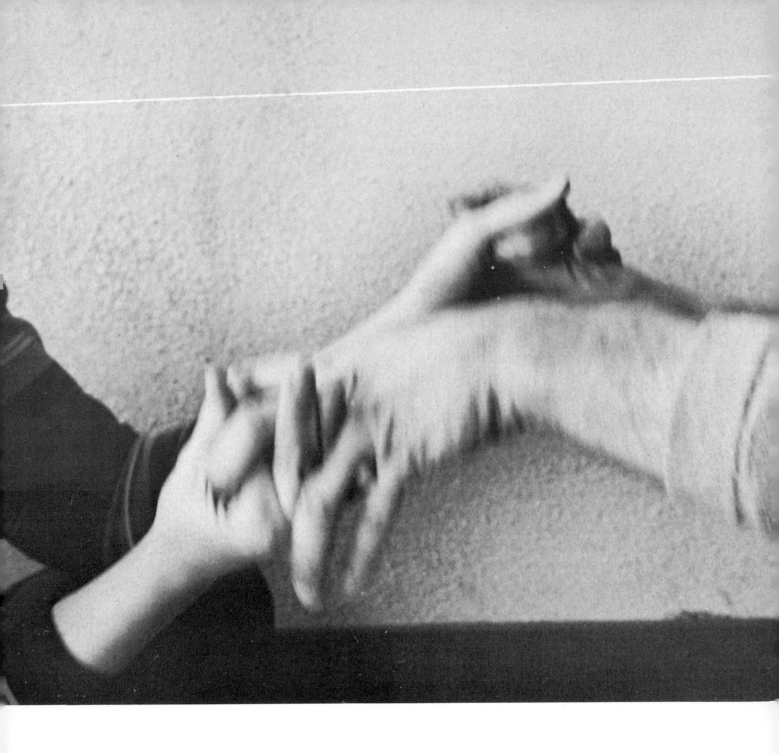

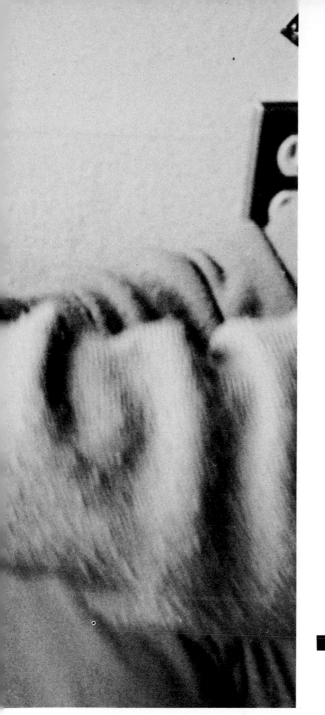

play (because it's fun)

for the **sun**

H

C

A

E

R

It's not very far.

SONG

1. Just another rainy Sunday
   Sittin' in my room.
   Just a day like many others
   Sittin' here alone.
   Close my eyes
   And wish
   That I
   Could be a child again.
   Be a child again.

Children: Come with us.

Take a walk outside with us.
Feel the rain against your face.
Jump a puddle,
Throw a pebble
And laugh . . .
Until you know,
There is no such thing
As just another day.
Just another day.

2. Just another normal Monday
   Draggin' off to work.
   Just a day like many others
   Traffic, crowds, and clocks.
   Close my eyes
   And wish
   That I
   Could be a child again.
   Be a child again.

Children: Come with us.

Come outside and play with us.
Swing so high you seem to fly.
Let the grass
Caress your feet.
Tumble, roll
Until you know
That there's no such thing
As just another day.
Just another day.

3. Just another tired evening
   Watching the TV.
   Johnny Carson talks and laughs
   With bright celebrities.
   Close my eyes
   And wish
   That I
   Could be a child again.
   Be a child again.

Children: Come with us.

BOTH: Feel the night air
See the stars.
You can dream
You were on Mars.
Hold her soft hands,
Dream your dreams
And laugh . . .
Until you know
There's no such thing
As just another day.
Just another day.

Close my eyes
And wish
That I
Could be a child again.
Be a child again.

Children: Come with us . . .

You can't work creatively
Until you've learned to **p·l·a·y**.

imaginary ball

Everyone stand in a circle. Hold the imaginary ball in your hand. Throw it into the air. Higher and higher. Bounce the ball. See how high it bounces! Bounce together. Throw the ball high, higher. Open your mouth very wide. Catch the ball in your mouth. Swallow it. It hits your stomach and bounces. Now it's bouncing inside you. It makes you bounce. Bounce.

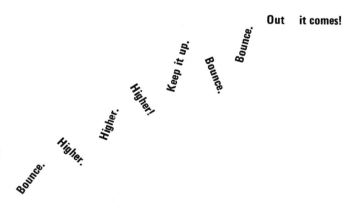

Bounce. Higher. Higher. Higher! Keep it up. Bounce. Bounce. Out it comes!

fantasy

is

PLAY

of the

highest order.

TO A CHILD

"small wonders,"
small wonder
"often escape the eyes of
full grown people
busy with
everyday
groveling for progress
and roots
without seeing the sky
or kissing stuffed toys
or each other."

small wonders
fly by as
firsts, onces
and most often never agains
missed
because the small world
really is
for most of us
caught up in jobs
and home repair manuals
or Sears catalogues
containing everything
but . . .
small wonders.

like today
tonight
and yet most beautiful
tomorrow
for friends
and singing
or dancing in the living room.

"teach me,"
small wonder,
"to see."

I am me
I am just me
I am a little like other children
But mostly,
I am just me.

-Mark Giloni
Age 11

on the pole

For groups of twelve or less.

When played by a group of trusting persons, this exercise can be a great physical relief and source of learnings. Get a pole about eight to ten feet long. A wooden clothes pole or a 1½-2" diameter pole will do. Lay it on the floor or the grass in the middle of the group, which stands in a circle around it. The instructions are to do with the pole whatever you want. As many can become involved as care to. The only rule is play fairly and be careful. The pole exercise will reveal such things as the subgroups which have formed and the individuals who are asserting themselves. Before the Control and Intimacy questions have been faced and dealt with, it is likely that a lot of counterforce of the Win/Lose, Lose/Lose variety will appear. Do not use this exercise if you are not trained or prepared to deal with conflict. You may do more harm than good. After intimacy has been reached, the pole is a good device to use as an instrument of play.

You may want to follow play on the pole with a free-form group dance, touching hands only. Stand in a circle and touch the tips of fingers rather than holding hands. Move in any manner that the group chooses.

animal play

Get down on all fours, and make an animal sound. Crawl around and greet the other animals. Nudge them, play with them.

SONG

Chorus: Right now livin'
        Is the only kind
        You know.
Yesterday, tomorrow stuff
        Nothing you can do.

        Right now livin'
        The only kind
        You know.
Good times, bad times
Only once times times
        Only!

1. Sitting on the floor
        Build a crazy zoo
For the plastic animals
        To be in
        Eat in
        Right now.

2. Silly sorta books
That leave you cold
        Get warm
        When she reads
        The words clearly
        Slowly, only.

Chorus: Right now livin' . . .

3. Hold her close
'Cause she wants you to
        And so do you.
        Preoccupied?
Nonsense work.
        Hold her only.

Chorus: Right now livin'
        The only kind
        You know
        . . . .
Good times, bad times,
Only once times times
        Only!

free play

Any group of any size can go wild together and discover the sheer joy of play. After the experience, the exhilaration remains. Everyone hold hands and go outdoors. Although a lot of learnings could result if you wanted to take the time to talk about it, why not just enjoy the experience? Set a time for the experience so participants have an idea how long the experience will be. Attempt to maintain unity with each other during the experience. Free play requires total participation. Everyone's in. Avoid intimidation by not having any observers.

Run together. Jump together. Scream together. Do whatever together means to your group, holding hands the entire time. The hand holding rule will encourage unity.

This will probably not work as a group starter, but is good after groups have been together for some time.

VARIATION: Have small squares of colored construction paper on a table. Red, yellow, blue, green, purple, and orange are about all you will need for a large group. This exercise is a good way to start a weekend and is not recommended for short meetings.

Each person picks a color from the choices. The choice should be a color which is significant to them, and not a random choice. The groups are formed by colors. All the reds together, all the purples together, and so forth.

Set a time for the play, go outdoors and engage in free play. The group hold hands in order to maintain unity. Run. Jump. Scream. When the groups return, talk about the experience. Did it help to bring them together? Play can be a good starter. Do not be deluded into thinking that this kind of play indicates that there is no more to be done in getting to know each other. This is only the beginning. At the end of a weekend together, you may want to repeat the exercise, and experience the difference.

What can we say about spring
That hasn't been said before?
Buds bursting
Yellow flowers
Forsythia
Daffodils
Tulips and crocuses
Sleeping trees
Waking from winter
Naps
And cold rest
Seeds flying
Annual happening
Nothing new in all that
Can be said
But
I feel renewed
And WOW!
So much a part of it all.

One day you'll be free
And so will I.
We'll take a breath of fresh air
And breathe it in.
Someday nobody will be full of guilt.
We'll all be free as the birds.
We can fly.

-Laurie Persons
Age 10

HOW LONG HAS THIS BEEN GOING ON

On just a day
Like other days
I looked in my backyard.
I saw
It seems
For the very first time
How much alive
Was really there.

How long
Has this been going on?
It must be new
How long can it last?

As long
As the grass grows
And mankind knows
His place
In this place.

On just another
Rainy day
When clouds and air hang heavy
Holding everything in
I looked.
It seems
For the very first time
Saw black smoke against the sky,
Smelled the sulphur air,
Was it really there?

How long
Has this been going on?
Too long.
Is there no place
In this place?

As long
As the grass grows
And mankind knows
His place
In this place.

111

foot circle

All the participants remove shoes and socks. Put them into a common pile. Touch feet in a foot circle. It might be appropriate to talk about it in terms of holding feet. Enjoy it.

right now

There is nothing you can do about this morning this afternoon. Nor is there anything you can do about what will happen this evening or tomorrow as a matter of fact.

Right now is the only time that matters.

Right now is good.

Right now someone needs you. It's never convenient. You always seem to have something to do, even if it's nothing.

Right now she wants you to read a story, or make love. Right now is the time to build a block zoo. Right now is the time to talk long on the phone. Right now you're needed. To listen, or hold hands, or cry, or laugh, or be.

Right now someone needs you, not later because your shoes are off and you're tired or hassled.

Pssst . . . . There's a footnote. Right now living can get you conned. Someone didn't need you . . . really. It was all a fake to get you.

But right now is still the only place to be. Cynics get conned too and miss all the fun of the good time or the emotional weight of bad time.

Relax! There's nothing you can do about this morning, this afternoon. Right now is the only time that matters . . . really.

The**dark**night is ended.

We can see the SUN.

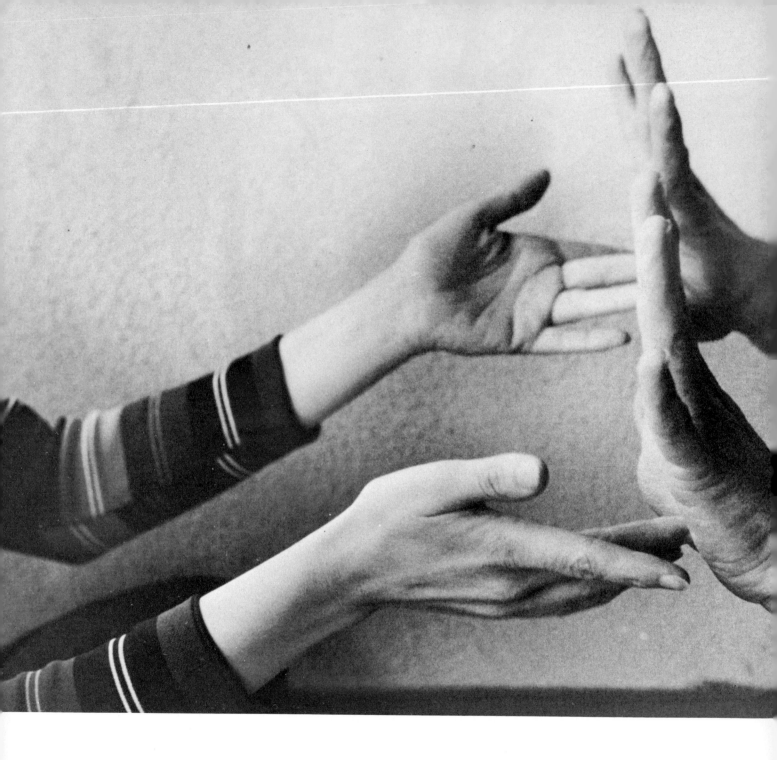

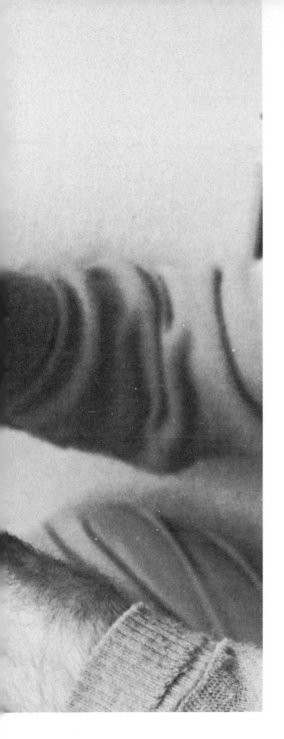

again

for such a very long time
the Clown
wished to be a dreamer.

his round face
that looked like
so many others
would become long
and handsome.

his eyes
deep-set
thoughtful
far away
in clouds.

a not very special
body
tall and lean
angular and strong.

maybe even a king.

His Queen
And Noble Children
Growing Happily
Laughing
Together.

For Such a Very Long Time
the chalk white face
and painted
real tears
were covered
By Tanned and Noble
Make-up.

He Dreamed
His Kingdom
His Future
His Present
Tense.

it blew away
one day in the storm.

the queen laughed
the children
scorned
their jester.

for such a very long time
the Clown
wished to be a dreamer.

the king is dead.
Long Live
The Clown.

The more things change,
the more they appear to remain
the same.

THE NEW HOUSE

The new house
Is big and
A bit intimidating.

Here we are in the
Middle
Of a dream
And it feels like
The Holiday Inn.
Nice
But not home.

The new house
Makes us feel
Far
Apart.

The new house
Is breaking
My back
And hers.

New houses
Have a
Way
Of doing that
To people
I guess.

They reach
Out.
Grab
You into them
And challenge
You to make yourself
Welcome.

You're a stranger
Here
And not too
Awfully together
Because
You're strangers
In the same house.

THE PLAY WENT SOUR

I don't know why the wall went up.
We sat together on the river bank
Watched clouds
Shaped like dreams
And laughed
When we discovered
We could still whistle
Blades of grass
Between our thumbs.

I don't know why the wall went up.
We flew a kite with a knotted tail
Let out the string,
Sent paper messages to the gods
And ran
Until we fell
Exhausted
By the chase
When the string broke.

I don't know why the wall went up.
We sang old rock songs
With three chords
Until we were hoarse.
Then talked
Or whispered sadnesses
So deep
Our eyes were red with tears.

I don't know why the wall went up.
It's there
Only for the moment.
Our trowels were always there
Secreted in our back pockets
Ready to build new walls.

I don't know why the wall went up.

Let's sit together on the river bank,
Whistle grass between our thumbs,
And laugh again.

121

WINTER SOLSTICE

Ever try to keep a life-sized
Raggedy-Ann
Standing strong and firm
And straight?
Especially when
All the time you felt
Like Raggedy-Andy.

Know what?

It doesn't work.
As long as you keep thinking
It's Raggedy-Ann you're holding
And you feel like you're Raggedy-Andy.

You get to a win/win life-style, having busted your you-know-what working through the concrete wall called control questions and come out on the intimacy side. Well, maybe you're not through it and took another route, over, under, or around. But anyway, there you are, thinking you're through it and your face is pressed tight against it again.

You're down. Way down because of the effects of planet positions, the sun and the moon at the winter solstice, or maybe because you didn't ever play the Christmas game well and the tree cost more than you could afford. Many reasons why. But you're down.

Down and can't get a handle on what it is. Guilt. Anxiety. Uptight. Stomach in knots. Even the groovy exercises aren't helping. So is she. Way down. Mope around. Drag each other down.

Then it hits you. So simple. Should've thought of it before. You're down. She's down. Both down. Not the first time or the last.

Then you remember. What it was you wrote in blood before. Don't need this win/lose, lose/lose stuff. You can lift the other up using all your strength because you trust she'll do the same. And there's no way I'm Raggedy-Andy because I know she's not Raggedy-Ann.

Planets beware!
Sun!
I don't care where you are.
Moon!
Watch out!
We're here
And there's no stopping us.

Noah!
Guess you knew
All along
That
Arks can be built
In spite of zoning ordinances
In the neighborhood.

You were right.
All you people
Who never let
The winter solstice
Wipe you out.

Christmas tree salesmen!
Here we come
Watch out
Plant ten more
Because
Our children are coming too.

Watch out moon and stars
We're moving toward
The center
Of each other
Where we want
To live
Together.

MY HOUSE IS BURNING DOWN

If your house is on fire, do you
Stay in the building and let the
Burning pieces fall in on you or
Do you leave and come back
After the fire has destroyed the house
And begin to rebuild it.

Funny how the rain
Makes things clean all over again.
Like starting out fresh
With no history
To speak of.
Rain washes the dirt
Of the world
Away down the drain
To the sewers
Where even the rats
And the cats
Can bathe.

Funny how the rain
Makes things clean all over again.
It rained
In the garden
As they left
To find greener pastures
To raise their children
Away from the prying eyes
Of the magician
Who made everything
Possible,
And time a probability.

Funny how the rain
Makes things clean all over again.
In the streets
Where yesterday
Exists only in the hangover fog
Of the man in the gutter
Rising to another day
Fresh
To the store to buy another
Foggy afternoon
Of fuzzy
Probability.

Funny how the rain
Makes things clean all over again.
In the depressed caverns
Of my mindful
Wanderings
Around my life and
Contemplations of my death
Or even last weekend
When everything was clear
For one whole day.
Dreams of comfortable reality.

Funny how the rain
Makes things clean all over again.
Except the news
And my car
Dirty from the winter
Long dark dreary winter
Coats and slushy snow
Down the drain.
Rain
Wash my brain,
My hands,
My face,
My car,
My past,
My now, my tomorrow
Rain again tomorrow
Make things clean all over again.

Funny how the rain . . .

Not funny at all,
Or even the slightest bit unusual.

EVIL SPIRITS I HAVE KNOWN

Love?
I don't know what it means
Really.

Strive for this
Above all others.
Be without it
Life is empty.
But my life is full
And I don't know
What it means
Really.

Incidentally,
I love you
Flipply
Shouted out
The rolled-down car window
Driving away
When I really wanted him to stay.
Love?
I don't know what it means
Really.
When I needed him to care
He drove away.

I love you
Her body
Warm and motion
Next to me
Childhood fantasies
Of harem girls
Never satisfied
She cried
I love you so much
I could scream
But the people in the other room
Would hear.
Simple joyful
Laughing.
Nothing wrong with that.
A beautiful hour.
Love?
I don't know what it means
Really.

Stay with me
And care for me
Tie yourself
To me alone.
Promise only
That we will try
Not to kill each other
Caring.

Jesus Christ
I don't know what it means
Really.

Life together.
Does that really mean
Forever.
Higher love?
It doesn't seem to work.
Levels of love
Won't fly either.
One at a time
For a life
One life
One love
No way.
Most of the time
Maybe
Love?
I don't know what it means
Really.

But I'll stay
With no strings
For as long as I survive
And as long as you want
Me.

Never will I drive away
Shouting
Incidentally
I love you.
The most I can say
Is I'll be back . . .
I think.

FINAL PRAYER

Lord,
Give us peace now.
Lord, give us peace now
Quiet later
We won't ask for more.

Let us love and feel
Joy
And tears
And warm bodies
Children laughing
Songs of
Living
Peaceful dying
Ride the many tracks
Enjoy the noise.

Just give us
Peace now
Peace now
Peace now
Quiet later . . .

And if it don't work out . . .

We still won't ask for more.

ADDITIONAL RESOURCES

Gunther, Bernard. *What to Do till the Messiah Comes*. New York: Collier Books, 1971.

Pfeiffer, J. William and Jones, John E. *A Handbook of Structured Experiences for Human Relations Training*. Vol I (1969), Vol. II (1970), Vol III (1971). University Associates Press, P.O. Box 615, Iowa City, Iowa 52240.